A 31-Day Leadersh

FOOTNOTES

From The Best Selling Author of *The Queens' Legacy*

KATRINA FERGUSON

Foreword by Renowned International Speaker, Les Brown

FOOTNOTES
A 31-DAY LEADERSHIP GUIDE FOR WOMEN

Cover design by: GreeneHouse Media, Print Division
Website: www.GreeneHouseMedia.com

ISBN: 978-0-9828180-0-8

To contact the author:
Katrina Ferguson
c/o FIG Publishing
12138 Central Avenue, #464
Mitchellville, Maryland 20721
1.888.202.6766
www.FIGPublishing.com
info@FIGPublishing.com

Footnotes

Aching arches, tired toes

Heels that carry all of your woes

Calves of courage, thighs of strength

Hips that sway with confidence

Laces or buckles, high heel or flats

When adversity approaches simply tighten your straps

Matters not if printed or solid in color

Ladies lead like no other

Some pairs are worn out, some new and still tagged

Luck favors the prepared so pack your shoe bag

Your passions and purpose, you must pursue them

If the shoes don't fit... simply grow into them

Mel Roberson

This book is dedicated to my amazing daughters Denise, Kianna and Kristyn.

Those who are greatest among us are our servants. The purest way to serve is through allowing the seed of leadership that God has placed in each of you to blossom and being obedient first to the 'leadership guide' that God has written on your hearts.

Live on purpose. Do destiny.

Be all God has called and created you to be.

Put on your leadership shoes and dance your way into your greatness knowing that no matter the challenge or the situation, you can dance anywhere . . . even if it's only in your heart.

TABLE OF CONTENTS

FOREWORD
INTRODUCTION

FOREWORD

Katrina Ferguson is an incredible mother of three beautiful daughters. She is a Speaker, Author, Trainer, and Entrepreneur. I am proud to call her my friend and business partner. She is also the author of *Footnotes - A 31-Day Leadership Guide for Women*. This book is a personal manual on how to leverage your leadership skills to have success in a fierce and competitive market. Do you need to know which direction to go as you endeavor to lead others into achieving personal greatness? *Footnotes* will help you to take your leadership skills to the next level. You will learn what it takes to strengthen your leadership and thereby increase your finances and enhance your career.

Katrina Ferguson takes you on a journey of shoes, if you will, an exploration into the world of shoes and how they symbolize specific leadership characteristics that we all must have. After all, shoes are the very foundation on which our feet rest. They are the vehicles used to protect our feet, symbolizing direction. *Footnotes* will force you to ask yourself probing questions that will allow you to determine where you are, where you intend to be, and how you will get to your next level of greatness. Katrina will teach you to reexamine your path and what you are wearing on your feet, so that you can be a forerunner, rather than a side-liner. In our society, in order to be successful, it is critical that you lead with passion, persistence, and preparation.

Footnotes will allow you to aggressively sharpen your leadership skills, maximize your effectiveness, and synthesize your ability to create and lead successfully. *Footnotes* will usher you to new levels of achievement and stretch you beyond your limits. Get ready to go and lead where no stiletto has gone before and make your mark in an industry that will be remembered for years to come!

THIS BOOK WILL CHANGE YOUR LIFE!

Les Brown
Speaker/ Speech Coach/Author

INTRODUCTION

Women are natural-born leaders. Period.

Now that we've established who we are, let's take a look at how and why we do what we do; and what skills we need to have to lead others effectively.

(Defn.) Leadership: (noun) The ability to influence people.

"Leadership is the capacity to influence others through inspiration, motivated by passion, generated by vision, produced by a conviction, ignited by purpose."

– Dr. Myles Munroe

'The difference between managers and leaders is that effective managers do things right, while successful leaders just do the right thing.'

~Peter Drucker

Look around and it becomes obvious that God planted the seed of leadership in each and every one of us. I'm sure some of you are saying, 'Oh no, not me; I'm not a leader. I can't lead anything and I don't want to lead anybody.' Well, like it or not - you are a leader; it's inherent in who you are and how you were made. You have been designed, equipped and destined to lead since the day you were born. It is time for you to walk into your God-given destiny.

Whether you're leading your family, your children, your congregation or your employees, you are called to be a leader. Intrinsic in leadership is the fact that if you're leading, then someone is following you; otherwise, you're just taking a walk. Hopefully, you're moving with purpose and someone committed to that purpose is following you. Take an objective look at your life and consider: Who's following your leadership and where are you leading them?

Traditionally, women leaders have gotten a bad reputation. Somehow our society has misconstrued strength, confidence, assertiveness and determination in women and equated those traits with anger, bitterness, rebellion and arrogance. Nothing could be further from the truth. In actuality, women leaders face all the challenges, obstacles and pitfalls of leadership that men do – often with the added pressure of societal expectations to still fulfill the traditional roles of wife, mother, caretaker, homemaker and volunteer – effortlessly and graciously without the slightest hint of weariness, fatigue or complaint. I think this quote made popular by Reagan senior White House staffer Faith Whittlesey says it all, "Ginger Rogers did everything that Fred Astaire did, except backwards and in high heels."

When it comes to true leadership, we're not talking about the bossy, menacing, overbearing, trying-to-sell-a-used-car-at-any-cost type of leadership. We're talking about the attractive, compelling and inspirational type of leadership that makes people want to go where you're going – just because you're leading the way.

It's All About the Shoes

So what do shoes have to do with leadership? It's all about style.

We've outlined a month's worth of shoes and leadership qualities that every woman needs to have. Wearing the right shoes, just like navigating through life, projects certain qualities and sends certain messages in the process of accomplishing specific goals. Join us on this journey as we Celebrate the Power of Shoes!

There is a shoe for every mood, every moment, every emotion and every attribute. Shoes are a symbol of who we are as women; what we feel, how we think, what we want. You can look at a woman, then at her shoes, then at her face and know almost everything that's going on with her at that moment. Shoes are an extension of who we are and how we connect with the world around us.

Here are 31 pairs of shoes and 31 leadership traits every successful woman needs to have in her physical and emotional closet.

SHOE BOX # 1
Wedges & Moderation

Wedges made their original debut in the 1970s on the feet of female leading ladies on television and silver screens around the world. They re-entered the fashion scene in the late 2000s and have become a wardrobe staple in the closets of teens, tweens and professional women around the globe.

Wedge heels run the entire length of a shoe and take up the entire space under the arch and heel of the shoe. In contrast to most high heels, wedges actually create a sense of stability and comfort while walking; in addition, they are appropriate to wear in casual and business settings.

Just like a comfortable pair of wedges, every woman needs to find a good emotional balance between flats and high heels; hence, moderation.

Even the Bible encourages its readers to seek moderation in all things. Why? Because balance is one of the keys to a successful and enjoyable life, and over-the-top leadership can be ineffective and turn off potential followers.

Moderation enables you to avoid extremes. It's the ability to be heard between a yell and a whisper, and to command the attention of a room by hitting just the right note and speaking in just the right tone to get and keep the attention of the audience.

The woman leader who operates in moderation is not prone to overreact or react in extreme fashion. When she receives bad news or needs to respond to a crisis, she doesn't allow her emotions to dictate her response. She understands that her emotions are a signal to warn of impending danger, not a tool for decision making. When the pressure is on and everything is on the line, a wedge-inspired woman knows how to release her pressure valve, blow off a little steam, and stay the course. A leader influenced by moderation keeps her cool and allows reason to lead the way while traversing the uncertain paths to her ultimate victory.

SHOE BOX # 2
Cleats & Tenacity

Cleats are most commonly seen and most frequently utilized in athletic environments and extreme sporting events like hiking, mountain-climbing and rappelling. Cleats feature studs on the bottom of shoe soles to help gain traction on smooth, slick or slippery surfaces – and to assist in rapidly changing directions when it's necessary to quickly alter a plan or change courses; something every effective leader must know how to do.

For female athletes, cleats are most often used in soccer and mountaineering where grassy fields and steep rock faces present challenging surfaces for the athletes to maneuver on uncertain terrain.

Have you ever heard the phrase 'she has the tenacity of a bulldog?' Well, in some circles, that's actually considered a compliment because it means the fearless leader has the ability to dig her heels into something (e.g. an idea, a cause, a dream or a goal) and not let go until she gets what she wants. Tenacity is close kin to persistence and dogged determination;

demonstrating the ability to dig deep and hold on tight in relentless pursuit of her target.

Tenacity is required to get things done. As any real leader knows, there will always be obstacles and naysayers who offer 1,001 reasons why something can't be done. There will always be someone who says an idea or task is impossible to accomplish. There will always be detractors who believe that the status quo is just fine and there's no reason to think beyond the way things are 'because we've never done it that way before.'

So, cleats off to the women of substance who know how to think and act outside of the box. Women who know there's a better way, and that if they get clear on the reasons why they have committed to a certain task, how to do it will take care of itself. Cheers to the bulldogs in the boardrooms who know that anything worth having is worth fighting for until the bitter, better end.

SHOE BOX # 3
Dancing Shoes & Passion

Put on your dancing shoes, we're going out tonight! That's the clarion call for a night filled with fun, excitement, adventure and a passionate love of life.

Roger Vivier, the famed French fashion designer who is most noted for redesigning, reviving and reintroducing the world-famous stiletto to A-list fashionistas is quoted as saying, "To wear dreams on one's feet is to begin to give reality to one's dreams."

When you think of dancing shoes, images of ballroom, salsa and open-toe sandals with ankle straps come to mind; a shoe that's ready to Rumba the night away.

When you think of passion, what comes to mind? Raw, unbridled emotion. A zest for life. True belief, commitment and dedication to a cause – unequivocally.

The best career advice I ever received was, 'Do what you're passionate about, and the money will come.' I do, and it does.

Passionate leaders aren't afraid to throw caution to the wind every now and then and wear their hearts on their custom silk sleeves. It's that type of enthusiasm, gusto and drive that has the ability to incite activity and excite followers and fans to join together for a common cause.

Passion is what keeps the engine running when reality sets in and things don't go as planned. Passion is what makes a dream or goal worthwhile when the bank account is low or the cash flow isn't that steady. Passion is the lifeline that resuscitates an idea long after the life support systems of logic, reason and rationale have faded. Passion is what makes it all worthwhile in the end.

What are you passionate about? What are your dreams? What does it take to make them come true? Create the strategies, do the corresponding activities and live your dreams. Most of all, avoid procrastination. Procrastination is the arch enemy of passion. Procrastination is devastation. It is the assassination of our destination. Our mantra must be, "I will do it now." Remember, inch by inch, it's a cinch. By the yard, it's hard. Just start moving in the direction of what you want and remember that baby steps count. Go for it!!

SHOE BOX # 4
Cross Trainers & Adaptability

Cross trainers: what a novel idea. They're the perfect shoe for running, walking, aerobics and various court sports.

Cross trainers have been pegged as the all-around workout shoe and the ultimate footwear for all-things-athletic. You can visit any court, track, walking or hiking trail, city sidewalk, aerobics studio, field or stadium and find cross trainers in action. Cross trainers are designed with functionality in mind. Shoe manufacturers have invested a lot of time and money understanding how the human body responds to the pressures inflicted by moderate to intense exercise. Cross trainers are designed for flexibility and shock absorption to minimize impact under stress... much like good leaders.

A good leader is like a good cross trainer: flexible, adaptable, adept. There are no "typical days" for leaders, because each and every day is unique in its own right; each day is filled with a variety of opinions, challenges, decisions, options and opportunities. Leaders have followers, so it's necessary for them to consider the impact of their actions and how everyone on the team is personally affected by their decisions.

Leaders understand that it is impossible to motivate other people to action. By definition, to be motivated means that an individual first must make a decision to move. Therefore, in order to move someone, leaders understand that they first must inspire them by engaging that person's own thoughts and ideas. This is why it is important for a leader's own source of inspiration to be cultivated and primed to generate sustainability for the duties ahead.

Leaders are required to influence others, but that influence does not come without responsibility – sometimes financial and fiduciary, many times personal and emotional. Leaders must make tough choices, some of which may be unpopular or impact others in less than optimal ways; others may be life-changing and leave an indelible print on the lives of many. Leaders are called to unwavering commitment to a vision, mission and purpose for which they must adapt and adjust to ever-changing circumstances. Yes, true leaders—like a good pair of cross trainers—are well-suited for the tasks at hand.

SHOE BOX # 5
Galoshes & Imperviousness

"Imperviousness" – now there's a word you don't hear every day when you're simply talking about shoes. But an impervious nature is something that you want both your galoshes and your leaders to have.

The Greek origin of galoshes initially referred to a heavy, wooden shoe or boot; then the meaning morphed into something of an "overshoe," to its modern-day definition of a heavy, rubber boot that repels water and moisture.

Galoshes aren't all business. What often comes to mind is bright yellow boots on the feet of children jumping over (or into) mud puddles and standing pools of water. Make no mistake, galoshes still experience the storm, they just aren't overwhelmed by it.

An impervious leader isn't without feeling, she just doesn't allow those feelings to penetrate and impede her ability to make good decisions. High-profile leadership positions often put the leader dead-center in a bull's eye; a target for every critic, detractor, opponent or rival. We've all heard the childhood adage, "sticks and stones may break my bones, but words will never hurt me." That's simply not true. Yes, sticks and stones can break your bones, but words can break your spirit.

Words can and do hurt, especially when they're laced with false accusations and half-truths that can undermine a genuine agenda. Words can hurt when they're unkind and unexpected – especially from an unlikely source. Words do hurt when they misrepresent the truth and mar someone's reputation and undo their hard work.

For most leaders, harsh words are an occupational hazard, so developing a thick skin (rather than sporting soft, baby's bottom skin) is part of their uniform and par for the leadership course. Being that this is in direct opposition to the theoretical thin skin women are born with—and encouraged to use to our emotional advantage—we must be more intentional about becoming thick-skinned.

An impervious nature allows a leader to get wet in the rain without getting soaked to the bone. This personality trait is a key leadership survival skill.

SHOE BOX # 6
Mary Janes & Inquisitiveness

Mary Janes. Not just any Mary Janes, black patent leather Mary Janes. Shiny, flirty, cute, curious, sweet, innocent. These are the Sunday favorites of my granddaughters.

Mary Jane, originally a character in the Buster Brown comic strip, has been around more than a century. The namesake shoes are a ubiquitous presence in the closets of most little girls and stir up memories reminiscent of the good ole days marked by simpler times gone by.

Traditionally, Mary Janes were known for their comfort; a low heel, soft sole and wide buckle that made walking a thing of ease. Mary Janes were the shoes of Christmas plays, Easter pageants, and the first day of school. Contemporary Mary Janes have experienced nothing short of a makeover. They are sexy, stylish and fierce, but in a sweet and unassuming way.

If you have children, then you are well aware that they can ask 'Why?' all day long. It's that eagerness to learn and never-ending curiosity that endears itself to the person being questioned. We need our leaders to ask, 'Why?' And we need our leaders to know 'Why?' As a popular leadership quotation states,

"The person who knows *how* will always have a job; the person who knows *why* will always be their boss."

An inquisitive nature in business and entrepreneurship leads to fresh, original ideas and new, innovative ways of doing things. Inquisitiveness also uncovers unproductiveness and inefficient methodologies. Asking 'Why' something has always been done a certain way can lead to new ways to accomplish the same thing with less effort and fewer resources.

Whether it's the low-heeled Mary Janes of the early 20th century or the high-heeled platforms of the new millennium, let's encourage our leaders to maintain their sense of curiosity, and let's encourage their inquisitive natures.

SHOE BOX # 7
Flats & Practicality

Flat shoes are sexier than they sound if for no other reason, than they accomplish the purpose for which they were created. Flats are the comfort-food of shoes; familiar, reliable, stand-bys that tend to fit like a glove and massage our weary feet. Flats are unpretentious - sturdy, durable. They just make sense.

We all know that high heels are killers on your feet, wreak havoc on your back and spine, and cause undue damage to knees and joints. But we don't really care, because they look hot. Flats never make those demands on us. They simply allow us to be who we are – unrestricted, unencumbered, and sometimes unimpressive.

Once, I had a co-worker who wore old, beat-up flats. For all intents and purposes, she was not outstanding in any particular area of her life. She was, shall we say... homely; a bit on the boring side. She was drab and predictable. Or maybe she wasn't, but her worn flat shoes spoke so loudly, I couldn't hear or see beyond them.

The truth is that flats actually can be cute or dressy – they just tend to mute the volume on whatever message you're trying to project. Sometimes that's just what the doctor ordered. Every day can't be red-bottom stiletto day. Every day can't be butt-kicking combat boots day. Every day won't be fuzzy bedroom/bunny slippers or barefoot day. There will be some days that you need to walk steadily and even-keeled into the flames of executive management, administrative staff, accounting or personnel and simply engage your extinguisher and put out fires all day. Although firefighting in heels is much sexier, it's just not practical.

Search out leaders who understand how to scale it up and tone it down when necessary. Model your own leadership style after the adaptability and flexibility of a woman who knows when it's time to lay aside the pumps and put on some flats.

SHOE BOX # 8
Platform Shoes & Balance

Don't have a soapbox on which to stand and make your case? Consider a pair of platform shoes. Unlike many other shoe counterparts, platforms were invented with the sole purpose to elevate the wearer. Ranging in heel heights from 3 inches to 9 inches, platform shoes have endured multiple resurgences in popularity fueled by sightings on various celebrities, entertainers, designers, models and personalities of fame or notoriety.

Platforms have made their mark across the footwear landscape, influencing shoes, boots, flip-flops, sandals, sneakers and clogs with their exaggerated soles and remarkable ability to steady the gait of the wearer. Even though most high heels tend to create unsteadiness and improper balance, platform shoes do just the opposite.

"Balance" is one of those overused buzzwords that gets thrown into conversations among women discussing 'How to have it all.' Not possible, some say. Yes, you can have it all – but not at the same time - others say. But the consensus is always the same: the key to life is BALANCE. Maybe, maybe not. I'm learning that a healthy, unbalanced lifestyle might just work for some of us.

Effective leadership requires that some things be out of balance. For example, the dry cleaning may just not get picked up – because the children have to be picked up first. And wouldn't most people be OK with a leader who gives 100 percent at work – even though she doesn't find time to start a new hobby or learn how to cook French cuisine? Most of us spend our lives decidedly out of balance; pursuing one particular dream or another to the exclusion of someone or something else. The challenge with balance comes in as we attempt to balance external forces over which we have no control. In my mind, the only balance that matters is the internal balance of spirit, soul and body. Once things are good on our inside, the outside is of no consequence. Stop waiting for someone else to put you on a pedestal. Climb up on your platform shoes for the purpose of being seen and heard. Each of us deserves our moment in the sun to take center stage and command the attention of an audience. At the end of the day, we should be able to find the much-needed stability we seek and the level of balance we desire. Leadership often means being out of balance to pursue what matters most.

SHOE BOX # 9
Strappy Sandals & Charisma

Strappy sandals are spring and summer night essentials. Just the mention of them elicits dreams and visions of midnight walks on a waterfront promenade or leisurely strolls with a significant other who probably won't notice or appreciate the extraordinary effort you've gone through to get an exact color match for the earrings and complementary Dolce and Gabbana (D&G) clutch to accentuate your entire outfit. But, I digress.

The name "strappy sandal" is fairly self-explanatory. The shoe is a cute accessory defined by its open-toe, sandal-like quality and multiple designer straps for dramatic flair and effect.

Would a serious woman of substance ever really wear a strappy sandal in a professional setting considering the historical and well-documented sexual connotations related to feet, toes and sexy sandals? Sure, why not. These sultry shoes exude confidence, charm, fascination and allure. That's the kind of magnetic appeal that savvy leaders want and use to their advantage.

Understand that there's a time and a place for everything. Strappy sandals most likely won't be welcome in the boardroom or the construction plan room, however, an after-dinner cocktail reception punctuated by wining, dining and schmoozing is a most appropriate setting for showing off pampered, well-manicured feet and toes.

Strappy sandals and the woman who wears them project charisma, confidence, self-assurance and style. A powerful and influential woman in a leadership role who can rock pumps, platforms, work boots, deck shoes and strappy sandals all in the course of one week shows that she has what it takes to fit in, blend in and adeptly handle any situation that's thrown her way.

SHOE BOX # 10
Mules & Versatility

Mules are backless shoes that have a closed toe. They can be cloth, leather, sequin or rubber, but no matter what shape, form or fashion they take, a mule, is a mule, is a mule.

The beautiful thing about mules is that they remain true to what they are – despite the unavoidable fashion trends that inevitably come and go. There are mules with low heels, high heels, platform heels, wedge heels; the list goes on and on. But nevertheless, at the end of the day, they are still mules. Versatile, yet reliably consistent.

Versatility is an invaluable leadership characteristic that is highly enviable. How awesome would it be to watch as your designated leader greets overseas guests in their native language; talks shop with the Information Technology (IT) staff about the newest upgrades in techno widgets and gadgets; crunches numbers with the accounting team in preparation for the upcoming audit; takes time to ask the cleaning crew about their weekend plans; volunteers to read a children's book during story time at a local daycare; makes it back to the office in time to pitch a new client; and then sends a text to her significant other just to say 'I Love You' and 'I'll be home for dinner'. That's versatility!

That's what you want in a leader... someone who doesn't lose themselves in the fray. The leadership job description dictates that it's often necessary to glad-hand donors, appease clients and constituents, and craft messages for the media. Knowing how to seamlessly and effortlessly flow from one setting to another is an invaluable skill.

Versatility is the ability to demonstrate competence across multiple disciplines and easily meander from one area of subject matter to another without losing focus or purpose. Versatility, like a good pair of mules in your shoe closet, is an indispensable characteristic that every leader should acquire and cultivate.

SHOE INTERLUDE:
"The Glass Slipper Scenario"

Who would have imagined that one of the most famous and enduring fairy tales of all times is about a shoe?

Yes, we've been led to believe that "Cinderella" is a story about true love, romance and redemption from those who've treated us poorly, however, those sub-plots are merely backdrops to the main character: a beautiful glass slipper that is the inspiration for the entire story.

Cinderella's glass slipper was the one thing she possessed that was uniquely her own. And when she lost it, she lost a piece of her *soul*. Fashioned out of a fairy godmother's magic wand, glitter and pixie dust, that one shoe serves as a constant reminder that even in the most unlikely set of circumstances, dreams can still come true. Pumpkin-turned-coaches and rodent-turned-stallions may be the stuff of fairy tales, but finding life's one true love is very real indeed. Maybe it isn't Prince Charming that you're in search of. Maybe you're looking for a career that you're passionate about. Maybe you're searching for a cause to commit to for your life's work. Or maybe you're looking to find out who you really are – to discover your potential and measure your true worth. Whatever it is you're looking for will fit you perfectly when you find it.

So, why was the prince so fascinated and taken by Cinderella's shoe? Surely, a man of stature and wealth at his station in life had seen exquisite shoes before. What was it about this particular shoe that captivated him so much that he called for an entire search of the whole kingdom to locate the owner of the slipper? It is because, like all good leaders, he had the ability to identify the gifts and value in others. The prince knew there was something special about this shoe and something extraordinary about the woman who was wearing it. The glass slipper represented the unexplored and unleashed potential in Cinderella's life.

Ironically, just like in the real world, you cannot commandeer someone else's dreams, talent or ability. The same way none of the other maidens were able to fit, force or squeeze their foot into the glass slipper, no one else can fulfill your goals and dreams for you; no one else can do what you do – the way you do it. No one else could dance like Michael Jackson. No one else has painted like Picasso. No one can truly be who they are not. In reality, we can only hope and wish upon a star that we are allowed to witness others' greatness in action.

When Cinderella and her glass slipper were reunited, there was no question about whether it really belonged to her, because it was a natural fit. The shoe posed no discomfort. There was a sense of ease in their reunion. Much like life, when you find yourself pushing, pulling and trying to force situations into existence, they're usually not supposed to happen. The thing you are most likely called to do is the thing that comes easiest to you.

Once Cinderella reclaimed her shoe, she was restored again; finding not only the part of her life that was missing, but also gaining true love. What is it that you're missing that fits you so effortlessly and naturally? My hope is that you do not spend your entire life in search of it, but that you would recognize and heed the counsel of others who see your strengths and talents and allow good leadership to bring you and your abilities together in purpose.

SHOE BOX # 11
Ankle Boots & Self Awareness

Someone wearing ankle boots is making a statement. They've forgone the simplicity of shoes, yet fallen short of the commitment to traditional boots, and donned ankle boots; a stylish and flattering go-between that accents the legs and adds a bit of pizzazz to an outfit.

Caution! Ankle boots don't work for every look and every body type. For example, they tend to shorten the length of the leg, making petite individuals or people of small stature appear even shorter. In addition, ankle boots tend to make wide legs and thighs look even wider, a look most of us are trying to avoid. The key to successfully pulling off ankle boots is to 'know thyself.' What look are you going for, and what statement are you trying to make? If you make a commitment to ankle boots, then you must know if you, with your body type, can pull off the skinny jeans or pencil skirt styles – combinations frequently paired with the chic booties. You must know what works for you.

A professor who teaches ethics at one of the nation's top universities often says to her students, "You need to know who you are before you have to prove it." Her point is simply that self awareness allows us to make better choices in our lives. The middle of a crisis is not the time to decide what you believe, or what causes and agendas you support. Self awareness requires a genuine consideration of all-things-self and an honest assessment of how you feel about situations and circumstances that might impact your company, your organization and/or your community.

Much like ankle boots, there are some things in this world that just aren't a good fit for you, and you need to know that in advance. Leaders need to learn their strengths and weaknesses and then endeavor to turn those challenges into opportunities. Spend time getting to know yourself so you can better understand and relate to others.

SHOE BOX # 12
Peep-Toe Pumps & Vision

Good leaders have great vision. We're not just talking about 20/20 vision, but also foresight and hindsight. They have the ability to see what could be – to know what's possible – and to turn dreams into reality. A leader's vision is often broad enough to incorporate many of the goals and dreams of those who choose to follow. They seem to have a panoramic view on all the issues, then somehow, make leadership look easy. There's an added bonus for the leader who can also turn up the heat and make it look good. A mentor of mine says 'there is only one degree difference between steam and hot water.' What's the lesson? We need to turn it up a bit, increase our vision, and as a result, enlarge our impact on the world.

Peep-toe pumps are cute, classy and stylish. For the most part, they are considered a business chic or formal shoe style. Peep-toes are dress shoes with a twist; boasting a small opening at the front which allows a flirtatious glimpse at the toes inside. The peep-toe revolution has asserted its influence on low heels, kitten heels, platforms and wedges. It's a traditional look that's all the modern-day rage.

Peep-toes were just pumps until the front cut-out added an element of vision that wasn't there before. So-so leaders are just smart or talented people moving from Point A to Point B until they have a vision that bonds a group to a common cause and purpose. Vision makes all the difference. Great leaders have great vision and purpose. Vision paints a picture of a destination and provides tangible proof that you're actually going somewhere that matters. If seeing is believing, then vision is the essence of existence.

McDonald's founder Ray Kroc and Disneyland creator Walt Disney were some of our nation's most talented visionaries. The creativity and passion they displayed toward building something that had never been done before inspired thousands of workers and billions of customers over the decades that joined the movement and bought into their visions. Activist and civil rights leader Dr. Martin Luther King Jr. envisioned a world of peace, equality and justice and inspired the world to unite and work toward that vision.

Great leaders have the ability to give those who are a part of their vision a glimpse into the future and inspire them to move toward their individual goals and dreams which have a part in the larger vision. True visionaries have the innate ability to see past what is right now and see into the realm of what could be – and what will be – if they simply inspire others to first dream and then work.

SHOE BOX # 13
Classic Black Pump & Common Sense

With so many types of shoes, colors, styles and options to make our feet look stunning, it's surprising that the classic black pump can still hold its own. However, some things simply never go out of style. The truth is that some things just make sense. Silver, polka-dot, jewel-studded platform shoes with an acrylic heel just cannot stand the test of time. Shoes like those are a fluke; a short-lived trend with no longevity.

The classic black pump is just a safe bet. At every interview, meeting, social outing or networking opportunity, the classic black pump is not only welcome, oftentimes it is embraced. Understated – maybe. Inappropriate – never. When in doubt about what to wear, consider a basic, yet classic, black pump, and you won't go wrong.

Have you ever heard the phrase by French author and philosopher Voltaire, "Common sense is not so common"? Unfortunately, he was right. If you look around the world today, it's hard to imagine what many people are thinking when it comes to the decisions they make about career, love or life in general.

Our society has been overwhelmed by a growing culture of self-entitlement, indulgence and greed which explains in part the social, economic and moral decline evident from coast to coast. The good news is that as a society, we can change. The bad news is that unless there are leaders who will stand up for what is right, we probably won't.

Where are the leaders who are willing to stand up for truth, justice and the American way? Where are the leaders willing to be the last ones standing while holding true to their convictions in spite of conflict or opposition? Where are the leaders who are willing to defend the rights of others who may be less fortunate or simply unable to defend themselves? Where are the leaders willing to forego what's comfortable or convenient; or popular and profitable; and pursue what's in the best interest of all? Where are the leaders committed to using common sense?

Often the leaders for our next generation can be found following the leaders of this current generation. Stated differently, in order to be a good leader, you first must be a good follower. Who are you following? Where are they taking you? And is that really where you want to go?

SHOE BOX # 14
Hiking Boots & Strength

Admittedly, hiking boots are not the most attractive footwear in the closet, but they are a well-kept secret with the ability to protect, defend and secure the feet of the individual wearing them. Hiking boots have a distinct role in that they are designed for navigating and withstanding difficult terrain. Their purpose isn't just for style or pomp and circumstance, their mission is to guard against the elements and anything else that might harm or injure the feet inside.

Hiking boots can be found on walking trails, hiking trails and mountainous ranges of the great outdoors. They're built to be sturdy, durable, reliable and weather-resistant, allowing the person wearing them to walk, run, hike or climb faster and farther in safety.

Hiking boots demonstrate a type of quiet and subtle strength that adds layers of protection people often take for granted. The soles are thicker to create a buffer and insulation against rocks or sticks on the path. The fabric is durable, yet porous, to protect the feet from outside moisture or blistering, while still allowing them adequate circulation for sweating and breathing. The interior lining adds padding for flexibility and comfort. And the construction of the boots supports the ankles to prevent breaks or sprains from uneven walking surfaces. Who knew hiking boots had so much to offer?

In comparison, who knew women leaders could carry the manifold responsibilities of career, marriage, family and community so effortlessly on their shoulders? After so many years of oppression and denial of rights; after centuries of being "less than" and generations of being denied access, who knew women were such strong and effective leaders? The answer is that we knew. We knew all along. We just needed the opportunity to prove it.

We owe our pioneering women leaders (and their boots) a lot for the sacrifices they made so that we would be in a position today to lead. We are indebted to leaders who didn't wait for permission to lead, but instead saw a need and intuitively stepped up to meet it. I'm talking about leaders like Harriet Tubman, who at the risk of her own life during the American Civil War era, led many others to freedom. It's well documented that although Ms. Tubman was a warm and sensitive woman, she had no problem telling someone that if they did anything to endanger the mission, she would shoot them. I believe she meant it, too.

Those seeds of greatness have been implanted in us since the beginning of time. The harvest is now. It's time for us to lead, follow or get out of the way.

SHOE BOX # 15
Bedroom or Bunny Slippers & Relaxation

What is it about a favorite pair of bedroom shoes or bunny slippers that can take the edge off of a less-than-fabulous day? Maybe it's their familiar comfort that allows you to ease into them without pretense or expectation. Maybe it's that slippers are non-judgmental. It doesn't matter if your feet are big or small, wide or narrow, if your toes are in need of a new coat of polish, or if your feet are due for a fresh pedicure. Fuzzy and comfortable slippers are inviting and send a message that says, "Come as you are. No advance notice or registration required." Admission is free with bunny slippers. No one is looking to see if your bedroom shoes match your robe, or if your bunny slippers are the latest designer brand. No one cares. The truth is that slippers offer a neutral fashion reprieve where you can simply relax and be yourself.

Although workaholic, Super-Mom, Type-A leaders are the stuff legends are made of, the truth is effective leaders understand that rest and renewal are as much a part of leadership as ability and zeal.

Take a moment to consider your own life. When you're tired, I'll bet you're just not as effective, not as productive, and not as good as you could be. It's a proven, biological and physiological fact that our bodies repair themselves while we're resting and sleeping. As a matter of fact, one of our greatest goals—weight loss—has been reported to only happen while we are sleeping. As soon as I heard that news, I went and took a nap! It's dangerous and destructive to fall into the cycle of 'all work and no play.'

What's unfortunate about our 24-hour workday and always-on accessibility through text messaging, e-mails and instant messaging is that we've systematically removed the much-needed time formerly set aside for rest and relaxation. The argument is that we have increased productivity, but at what cost? I'm inclined to believe that we are more creative and more productive when we've had time to "sleep on it." As a matter of fact, in the past, I found myself most productive when I would schedule a long weekend away from home, the kids, and all the associated responsibilities that accompany them, each quarter. Often when it seems like life is closing in on you, a simple long weekend can help make you sharper and make it easier to put everything back in perspective.

Let's banish the idea that relaxation is a bad word – and give ourselves a break. Take a vacation... you deserve it.

SHOE BOX # 16
Stilettos & Confidence

You know a confident woman when you see one. She doesn't need to say a word or validate anything she does. Her confidence (or in today's vernacular, her swagger) says it all. The woman who can pull off stilettos and take it all in stride is a modern-day marvel.

Stephen Bayley, a design critic and contributing editor for GQ magazine, was quoted as saying, "It is the flagrant lack of practicality that makes high-heeled shoes so fascinating." Yet it is the alluring look of that shoe that sends us on a quest for the ever-elusive comfortable stiletto. So, what exactly is this love-hate relationship we have with stilettos? On one hand, we love them because of what they represent. On the other hand, we hate them because of how they make our feet feel. Yet we wear them anyway because of the statement they make to others when we wear them.

At a glance, stilettos look like they're hiding a secret, while beckoning people to come closer and find out what it is. From a functionality standpoint, they lengthen the leg and make the calves appear shapelier and curvier. They also shorten the wearer's stride, tilt her forward and make her backside protrude ever so slightly. Stilettos are masters of flirtation and mystique.

It's fair to say that when women want to project sexy confidence and stylish sophistication, flats or loafers are not the answer. Rarely have I ever seen someone in a power suit or on a fashion runway successfully pull off a confident look wearing "sensible shoes."

Without question, girls, women and men are fascinated by high heels and stilettos. And it starts early. When my granddaughters play dress-up in my closet, they gravitate to my high-heeled shoes because the shoes represent a fantasy world in which they are confident women on the move, just like their glamorous grandmother or 'glamother' for short. Women know there's something magnetic and appealing about them that ignites the imagination and creates a sense of attraction and desire. Men love them for obvious reasons – and savvy leaders know how to tastefully use everything to their advantage. So, work your stilettos!

SHOE BOX # 17
Combat Boots & Assertiveness

Combat boots mean business. There's no mistaking the message being sent when a leader comes dressed and equipped for battle. Combat boots traditionally have been worn by soldiers on the path to war. They are practical, functional and purposeful in their design. Combat boots are constructed to provide ankle stability, grip and foot protection from rugged environments. Combat boots are notably unceremonious. When a leader shows up with their virtual or actual combat boots on, everybody knows that it's time to go to war and fight until we win.

There are several types of leaders. For example, there are autocratic, bureaucratic, charismatic, democratic and servant leaders – all with different styles, methods and approaches for how to get it done – whatever "it" is. They all utilize different strategies to fight the day-to-day battles and ultimately win the war. Depending upon the leaders' personalities and the motivation of the teams they're leading, each type of leadership has its pros and cons to measure effectiveness. But common in all leadership styles is the ability to be assertive when pushing a specific agenda.

Assertiveness should not be confused with aggressiveness, which is marked by overbearing, obtrusive energy or driving, forceful initiative. As an example, in the sales industry, an aggressive leader could be the one at the used car lot trying to stuff you into that lemon of a vehicle that may or may not make it off of the lot. You don't even have the opportunity to think through a decision because the salesperson is continually badgering and pressuring you to purchase the vehicle. On the other hand, an assertive car salesperson may be at a higher end dealership and will simply attract you to the car by sharing the benefits and details about the car, while painting a picture of how good you will look in that shiny, new ride.

Assertiveness is equated to bold confidence that respectfully impacts or influences others. Assertive leaders tend to cautiously choose their battles rather than allowing the battle to choose them. Quite often, I have to ask myself, "Is this the hill I'm willing to die on?" or "Is this a battle I'm prepared to fight?" I consider how fighting each battle will impact my overall effectiveness. In other words, is this a battle I *choose* to fight? Often, it is not. In those instances, the true strength and power comes in choosing to walk away. In other instances, it's time to tighten the laces on the combat boots and prepare to kick some gluteus to the maximus. In either case, we have the power to choose our battles, understanding fully that sometimes you have to be prepared to fight for what you believe in. Assertive leaders don't necessarily go looking for a fight, but they won't back down from one if it represents a cause they believe in or have a commitment to.

In my opinion, it's time to demolish the double standard for women when it comes to being able to confidently communicate a plan of action. Men are rarely called out of their names for being assertive – and the same should apply for women. There are times when we are put in a position to stand up for what we believe and we must be free to act passionately and professionally in those instances. Hats off to women who know how to assert themselves and therefore effectively lead their troops.

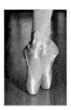

SHOE BOX # 18
Ballet Shoes & Talent/Skill/Ability

Ballet shoes are easily recognizable for their simplicity and ease of wear. The leather, canvas or satin lightweight slippers fit very closely to the foot to offer safety and flexibility for the dancer. Ballet shoes offer little in the way of support because in dance there's an understanding that the true source of strength belongs to the ballerina, not the shoes.

For advanced ballet dancers, there are Pointe shoes which help create the appearance of effortless, weightless dancing on one's toes. Again, the shoes offer little more than a padded toe box for strength or support, because the dancer is reliant upon her muscles to propel her into motion and move her across the stage. Based on appearance only, the flimsy tutus and whimsical attire worn during performances make ballerinas appear weak or frail; however, looks can be deceiving. Ballerinas happen to be some of the strongest athletes, dancers and performers there are. It is well noted that some football coaches and players use the stretches and strength training exercises of dancers to build muscle and increase endurance.

Ballet dancers and football players have as many similarities as differences. Both sets of athletes endure grueling practices under watchful taskmasters who ensure that they are disciplined and precise, demonstrating both mental and physical balance and control. In both cases, their careers can be cut short, even before they peak, at any age due to injury. Despite the commonalities of these performers and their routines, their environments are vastly different; ballet is fine wine while football is beer in a plastic cup. Can you imagine a football coach shouting, "Punt, Pass, Pile?!"   Ballet shoes, for all their simplicity, are on the feet of some of the world's top athletic performers.

There's a lot to be said about raw talent, skill or ability. Education is wonderful, along with pedigree, but no one can deny the wonder of a natural born leader. There are some skills that simply cannot be taught – no matter how much education, training or coaching is undergone. When Queen of Soul Aretha Franklin opens her mouth to sing, nobody in the audience questions what neighborhood she came from or which school of music she attended. It doesn't matter, because her raw talent speaks for itself.

Much like a skilled ballerina, the natural ability of a leader shines through on its own, leaving no question or debate about what she's capable of accomplishing. The beauty is that there are two schools of leadership: Born leadership and Developed leadership. Wherever you are in life, much like the ballerina, you can practice and become a skilled and effective leader.

SHOE BOX # 19
Clown Shoes & Sense of Humor

It's hard to look at a clown's feet and take him seriously. The brightly colored, oversized, floppy footwear is decorated with the intent of making everyone who sees them laugh. Typically, clown shoes feature an exaggerated length, with a two-inch bubble above the toes. The shoes are often vibrantly designed and festively customized with stripes, polka dots, zigzags, checks, bows or flowers.

Instantly, clown shoes and the humor that accompanies them are disarming. The shoes alone have the ability to bring a smile to the face of the most stone-faced audience; and definitely to kids of all ages. Despite their awkward appearance, clown shoes are comfortable and well-crafted for the amateur or professional clown.

It pays to remember that making people laugh is serious business, because laughter is an international language that connects us all.

It's evident that in business and in life, even more impactful than the right pair of shoes, is the right attitude of the leader who's wearing them. One of the quickest yet most effective wardrobe changes someone can make is to put on a smile... and learn to laugh.

Think about how at ease people feel around someone who's smiling and laughing. Immediately, the audience senses that the person is comfortable, which also puts others at ease. Seasoned leaders know the power of humor and that laughter can change the entire set of dynamics in a room. Although no one expects a leader to be a stand-up comedian, there is an expectation that she can put a crowd at ease and not take herself too seriously. Someone with the ability to laugh at themselves is often ahead of the game when it comes to getting what they want. Some of the actors and actresses that we are most endeared to are those that can laugh out loud, heartily at themselves, and especially in the middle of a performance. Comedy is a multibillion-dollar industry, which is a serious clue that our ability to keep people in the light-hearted space of laughter (not overdoing it, of course), is a pathway to successful leadership.

Scripture states that 'a cheerful disposition is good for your health; gloom and doom leave you bone-tired.' Psychologists, psychiatrists, physicians and the Bible all agree, laughter relieves stress, eases depression and promotes health. Indeed, it is the best medicine.

SHOE BOX # 20
Clean, Bare Feet & Honesty

Bare feet aren't just for babies. At some point in life, we all need the opportunity to kick off our shoes and feel the grass under our feet and between our toes. Bare feet provide a sense of freedom, wellness and emotional stability. Walking barefoot along the beach while listening to the roar of the ocean promotes peace, tranquility and clear thinking – sensations that are rarely found in the business and busyness of our lives.

People in bare feet also give the impression that they have nothing to hide. They've put it all out there for the world to see and tend to make others feel at ease. For some reason, it's easier to trust people with bare feet.

Winter, spring, summer or fall, bare feet don't go in or out of season. Like our best friends, they're just always with us. Though often hidden and tucked away under the newest fashion trends, our feet move us through life's ups and downs. Oh, the stories our bare feet could tell.

Understandably, we are limited in where and when we can expose our bare feet. They just aren't appropriate in most settings. We've all seen the signs warning us 'No shirt, no shoes, no entry.' Clearly, bare feet aren't welcome in a lot of establishments.

Bare feet are a metaphor for the honesty and transparency we desire in our leaders. They represent a genuineness and sincerity that reassures us into knowing that our leader knows what she's doing and we can put our trust in her. We want to believe that our leader is telling us the truth – even when it's difficult news or something we don't necessarily want to hear. Bare feet are symbolic of a fading past when someone's word was all that was needed to seal a deal; and a handshake was as good as a contract. Those days have long since passed, however the need for honest, true leaders who demonstrate true grit and trustworthiness have not.

Bare feet represent integrity and character and the ability to do what's right just because it's the right thing to do.

SHOE INTERLUDE:
"There's No Place Like Home"

Click. There's no place like home. Click. There's no place like home. Click. There's no place like home. Wouldn't it be wonderful if we could simply click our (high) heels together, repeat a particular phrase, and suddenly all our wishes and dreams came true? That was the case with Dorothy in "The Wizard of Oz," upon learning that her prized ruby slippers had magical powers to take her back home to Kansas after a mind-boggling, whirlwind journey through the Land of Oz.

So many leadership lessons can be gleaned from this film: The ability to attain true success is inside us all along; unity and strength are built through the bonds of friendship and encouragement; courage in the face of adversity; perseverance in the face of impossible odds; the power of positive thinking. And then there are other more subtle lessons like the pitfalls of hero worship; and the flaws and failures of pseudo-leaders like the Wizard. Not to mention that there are devious witches and Munchkins along the way whose sole purpose in life is to distract and deter you from completing your journey.

Have you ever heard the phrase, 'One man's trash is another man's treasure?' Well, that's evident in the case of Dorothy and her ruby slippers. Those shoes originally belonged to the Wicked Witch of the East before a house fell on her and killed her. The slippers are transferred to Dorothy by Glinda, the Good Witch of the North to protect Dorothy and her friends. Ironically, the tool that one individual used to create harm and destruction, was employed by someone else to prevent hurt and disaster – and ultimately to help an entire group reach their collective goals.

So far in this book, we've talked about 20 types of shoes and leadership qualities that successful women possess. All of them—in excess or moderation—can be used for something positive or exploited for something negative. The bottom line is although the shoes may make an outfit, it's the woman that makes the shoes. Dorothy's ruby slippers were neither good nor bad. They were magical shoes that fulfilled the wishes of the one who wore them. Think carefully as you put on your various pairs of shoes and be mindful to respect the high level of accountability and responsibility that comes with taking on a leadership role.

As a leader, in many cases people are entrusting their lives and livelihoods to you – convinced that your vision, ability and convictions will nurture, protect and keep them out of harm's way. It is your God-given responsibility to honor that commitment and faithfully fulfill the duties associated with your role as a leader. Throughout your journey toward greatness, you will encounter challenges and obstacles; and maybe even feel like quitting. The truth is that there are no magic, ruby slippers that can take you back home. But if you endeavor to valiantly lead and do the right thing – because it's the right thing to do – you'll find that those who've chosen to follow your lead will help carry you victoriously to the successful completion of your dream.

SHOE BOX # 21
Knee-high Boots & Power/Authority

In the fashion world, knee-high boots have been on the scene since the 1950s. They are a spin-off of their cowboy boots predecessor, and first cousin to the more rambunctious calf-high, knee-high and thigh-high go-go boots that were all the rage in clubs throughout the 1970s and Disco era.

Usually made of leather, rubber or synthetic fabrics, the purpose of knee-high boots is to protect the feet and insulate the legs. They are often accompanied by tights or long A-line skirts during the fall and winter.

In life, knee-high boots really come in handy when you need to tread into the muck, mire and deeper waters of business, negotiations, presentations, fundraising or sales. The leader wearing knee-high boots has come prepared to handle business, knowing there's a great likelihood that she will have to wade into the swamp of details to produce a desirable outcome (and income). Leadership requires preparation, and knee-high boots are just one more crucial piece of the wardrobe for someone who's not afraid to roll up her sleeves and get down in the trenches; working shoulder-to-shoulder with her team to accomplish their goal.

Whether we agree with them or not, the world gravitates to powerful leaders. They project an aura of respect and confidence that they have the knowledge, insight, experience and courage to get any situation under control. When it's time to make tough decisions, people don't feel very comfortable following an indecisive leader who seems unsure about what to do. Not only do we want our leaders to know what to do, we want them to tell us what to do – and make us feel good about doing it. Good leaders understand that they must exude confidence and control because their example sets the tone and standard for the entire team. Along with power comes authority which gives someone the ability and right to influence or command the thoughts, opinions and behaviors of others. Only a leader with knee-high boots in her wardrobe can pull that off successfully.

SHOE BOX # 22
Walking Shoes & Mentoring

When I worked in downtown Washington, D.C., I used to laugh at women who would forsake fashion for comfort and ride or stride into work carrying a pair of gorgeous shoes in their hand while sporting a pair of hideous "sensible walking shoes" on their feet. For years, I belittled their lack of commitment to the fashion cause and vowed to never fall into their unfashionable ranks and wear sneakers on the train as the completion of my professional suit ensemble.

Now I've seen the light. Fast-forward a few years, and I too have seen and learned the value of a good pair of walking shoes. No longer do I care about the judgmental fashionistas secretly snickering behind my back as I sport a pair of comfortable walking shoes. The truth is that I know something they don't know. I've been in this game long enough to understand which battles to fight and why. Having endured the pain of aching feet from shoes that were too tight, too high, and too impractical to actually walk in, I've learned the lessons and have been promoted to mentor status. The student has become the teacher; the mentee, the mentor.

Walking shoes are comfortable. They aren't always cute or stylish, but wearing them makes the whole day better. Something I often say is, "When your feet are hurting (even if it's only your little toe), there's nothing right in the world." Walking shoes are designed to fulfill the original purpose of shoes: to protect the feet. Walking shoes make no claims about helping you run faster, jump higher, make more money, fall in love, or land a multimillion-dollar athletic contract and endorsement deal. Walking shoes have no such ambition.

If a journey of a thousand miles begins with a single step, you absolutely will not make it without a good pair of walking shoes. Most of us just can't get far in 5-inch stilettos, but a good walking shoe can carry us through college, internships, first jobs, promotions, career advancements, business cycles, ups and downs, and various challenges over the course of our lives.

In times of confusion, challenge or decision-making, you know—the kind where you're pacing back and forth and going for walks so that you can think things through—a comfortable pair of shoes is necessary. Not only will a good pair of walking shoes get you there, but you'll arrive with all your faculties intact. Your attitude and your mindset will be right. You'll be prepared because you've had time to consider your steps rather than the pain of your feet. So, the next time you find yourself at a crossroads, put on a pair of walking shoes and 'walk it out.'

SHOE BOX # 23
Flip-Flops & Accessibility

I wonder who thought of flip-flops. Without question, when it comes to quality and construction, they are the Neanderthals of shoes, yet they persist. Flip-flops represent the baseline of footwear - offering little to no protection for the feet or ankles, minimal cushion and no structural support. Flip-flops essentially are "shoes" made of a thin rubber sole with two straps that join between the big toe and the next toe and connect to the side of the shoe on either side of the foot.

Flip-flips used to only be seen on sandy beaches in warm climates during spring and summer vacation retreats. However, their recent resurgence over the past decade has made them a ubiquitous presence in cities, malls, classrooms and college campuses around the world.

Since wearing flip-flops leaves nothing to the imagination, it's vital to make sure the individual wearing them has taken the necessary steps to take good care of his or her feet. Last summer, one of my friends was wearing flip-flops and I asked her if she had gotten a new job kicking powder! Lotion was definitely not her friend. Wearing flip-flops makes developing a good relationship with a pumice stone and foot creams a necessity. This means clean feet that have been moisturized and manicured; toe nails that have been trimmed or polished. Wearing flip-flops allows full access to one's feet, and we have to remember that other people are watching and judging us based on what we show them.

Although flip-flops aren't welcome in the majority of professional settings, the openness and accessibility they offer are. Yes, successful leaders need power, authority, decisiveness, confidence and assertiveness, but they also need to be accessible, lest they project an image of peering down from an ivory tower of privilege and foster a sense of disunity and disconnection from the people they've been chosen to lead and serve.

Much like the Wizard of Oz hiding behind a curtain and manipulating the lives of others through a veil of secrecy and inaccessibility, it's no longer acceptable for leaders to be far removed from the people whose lives they affect. The integrity of leadership means that we must be accessible and down-to-earth in order to be effective in the lives entrusted to us. Accessibility is equated with honesty and integrity; traits leaders must have to earn the trust of others.

SHOE BOX # 24
Golf Shoes & Patience

Do you really need special shoes for golf? The answer is yes. Golf shoes are made to stabilize players as they swing the club, provide leverage against the turf, supply traction, and help manage the shift and transfer of weight as golfers complete a full golf swing. Many courses also allow plastic cleats on the bottoms of golf shoes to improve grip on slippery grass surfaces.

Admittedly, from a distance, golf looks more like an exercise of standing around, waiting, talking and doing nothing, more than anything else; certainly not activities that require special shoes. But for the young leader in the process of building her career, she'll quickly learn that the game of golf is an example of the art and science of patiently waiting and learning to network and connect with other people while playing the game with the golf course as a backdrop.

Playing the game of golf is not for individuals in a hurry. Just as building a business or expanding a network doesn't happen overnight, successful leaders in the business of building and maintaining relationships understand that it too takes time. So even though it seems like you don't need special shoes or equipment for golf and the networking opportunities it provides, quite the opposite is true. It takes skill to keep someone's interest and engage them over the course of several hours. Keep in mind that communication is key when attempting to build rapport and find common ground.

Most often I find that a strategy for engaging people in conversation, especially individuals that you don't know very well, is to ask them questions about the people and the things they care about; causes or concerns important to them. Ask them about their families, their occupation, their reputation, their motivation; the acronym FORM for short. People love to talk about themselves. And when they're (finally) finished—because you listened and paid attention—they will become connected and endeared to you.

Traditionally, golf has been a male-dominated endeavor used to reinforce unity amongst the 'good ole boy' network. However, we are seeing more and more women on the golf course, in part, because that's where the deals are made. The networking that takes place throughout the day on the golf course plants the seedlings for the deals, opportunities and contracts that make up big business and open doors to new levels of leadership.

SHOE BOX # 25
Jeweled Slides & Uniqueness

Not everyone owns a pair of jeweled slides. They're more the shoes of fantasies and fairy tales that end with 'Happily Ever After.'

Wearing a pair of these savvy shoes allows us to showcase the unique characteristics or combination of traits that belong solely to us. Even though most leaders share a common skill set, there is something distinct about each individual, and it's important to share it with the world. When I think about jeweled slides, my thoughts turn to Queen Elizabeth, who uses her wardrobe as political leverage – making a statement through strategic style and coordination with her crowns and gowns.

These chic shoes are a combination of mules and sandals accented by a kitten heel, with the extra adornment of jewel-colored stones. They are in a category of their own, not really fitting the standard definition of loafers, sneakers or pumps. Jeweled slides need a place to project and make a statement – announcing their presence with a striking and bold confidence. These shoes are not for the meek, but for the leader who doesn't mind taking center stage and having all eyes on her.

What's unique about you? What story do you have to tell that can capture and engage the interest of others? What is it that makes you so special?

At first, most of us would answer saying that there's nothing really special about us at all. We're all wives, mothers, daughters and friends – working hard and trying to carve out our piece of the American dream. But there's more to us than that. There's more to you than that! Without question, you are more than your titles and your station in life. You are more than your academic degrees and life experiences. When it comes to you, the whole is greater than the sum of its parts. You are funny. You are kind. You are driven and focused and determined to leave your mark on this world. You are smart. And talented. Someone loves you, and their world wouldn't be the same without you in it.

SHOE BOX # 26
Tap Shoes & Decisiveness

Tap shoes are used in tap dancing, which every adept leader has theoretically had to do at some point in her career. Tap shoes have metal plates attached to the bottoms of the heel and toe sections of the shoes. The metal plates are called taps and make a loud sound when struck against a hard surface. Shoes don't make the taps; it's the taps that make the shoes in the world of dancing.

Tap shoes can be made from any type or style of shoe that has a bottom sole to which taps can be mounted. Tap dancers can perform almost anywhere, ranging from stages and arenas, to sideshows and sidewalks. Over the years, tap dancing has been featured everywhere from Broadway productions and jazz halls to ballroom studios and high school musicals. Tap dancing and tap shoes are versatile and mobile. The dance-shoe combinations are quick, intense and precise.

When we consider why a leader needs a pair of tap shoes, the ability to make quick and concise decisions comes to mind; to be in constant movement while keeping time with the rhythm of the moment. Often there isn't time to weigh pros and cons or gather a focus group and conduct user surveys. A leader should be well versed and well prepared at all times to make the best decision possible based on the information she has been given. Just like in tap dancing, every step is measured and amplified. If a shoe taps, people hear it. When a leader speaks, people listen... and respond.

On the other hand, there is also a need to "tap dance" around an issue. Euphemistically, we refer to that skill as diplomacy: the art and practice of conducting negotiations and skillfully handling affairs without rousing hostility; demonstrating tact. One of the best definitions I've ever heard for tact is by Winston Churchill: "Tact is the ability to tell someone to go to hell in such a way that they look forward to the trip." And Isaac Newton said: "Tact is the art of making a point without making an enemy."

SHOE BOX # 27
Running Shoes & Perseverance

When it comes to running the race of life and the perseverance required to do so, I constantly remind myself that although I have yet to reach my goal, I'm closer to it today than I was yesterday. With that thought in mind, it's much easier to continue running, regardless of the distance between where I am today and where I will be when I reach my goals and start living my dreams.

In America, getting a pair of running shoes has become a rite of passage. Known by many names: athletic shoes, trainers, gym shoes, sports shoes, sneakers and tennis shoes - a shoe by any other name is still a running shoe, the same. Whether high-tops, low-tops, mid-cuts or sneaker boots, the focus of a running shoe is on tread for maximum grip, side support to prevent the feet from rolling over, and flexible soles for maximum motion and maneuverability.

Running shoes were developed with endurance and stamina in mind. Running shoes are built to take the pounding of the pavement and endure in the face of obstacles like concrete, debris, rain and more. Several years ago, I ran the Marine Corp

Marathon – a total of 26.2 miles! As I took my place at the start/finish line, I did a last-minute inspection of my shoes to make sure they were tied properly and fit appropriately for the challenge ahead. I was not, however, concerned that my shoes would wear out or start to pinch my feet before the end of the race. Why? Because I selected my running shoes based on their ability to go the distance.

When we sign on to be a part of someone's vision, we sign on with the expectation that they're going to be there for the long haul. Vision statements are future-focused and used to help a group identify where they are now and where they're going. It's the leader's responsibility to help guide them to their ultimate destination. When it's time to start moving toward a vision, team members don't show up in high heels, sandals, clogs or flip-flops. They show up in running shoes – ready to go the distance.

SHOE BOX # 28
Sling-backs & Multitasking

Sling-backs are a pump-sandal hybrid. They are versatile shoes that range from casual to dressy to formal and may boast a low, medium or high-heeled sole. Sling-backs are characterized by the fact that they're backless shoes that offer a strap crossing behind the ankle or heel for support. Sling-backs have grown in popularity because they are appropriate for so many types of occasions and also are easy to wear. Sling-backs are a staple item in the multi-tasker's wardrobe.

I remember a time when "multi-task" wasn't even a word. I'm not sure what happened over the past few decades, but somehow women picked up the multi-tasker banner and have been waving it ever since.

There are countless books, seminars, websites and workshops on how to have it all and do it all; sometimes bit by bit, other times all at once. And since the height of the feminist revolution, multitasking has become the bane of women's existence.

Multitasking grew to fame during the Super-Mom era of the late 1980s and early 1990s that encouraged women to "bring home the bacon and fry it up in a pan," demonstrating the ability to perform multiple concurrent jobs or tasks; fulfilling old traditional roles of wife, mother and homemaker along with new non-traditional roles of breadwinner and provider.

Although the ability to successfully multitask has its benefits such as productivity and achievement, it's also fraught with drawbacks and pitfalls, often leading to an individual being overextended and overworked to the point of exhaustion. Many times leaders consumed by multitasking run the risk of becoming a 'Jack (or Jane) of all trades and master of none.' The key to successful multitasking is organization, decisiveness, the wisdom to delegate, and knowing when to say, 'No.'

SHOE BOX # 29
Work Boots & Dependability

We've all heard it said that the only place success comes before work is in the dictionary. Success is always preceded by work – as success must be earned. When you think about work, what often comes to mind is a dependable group of people day-in and day-out doing what it takes to get a job done. These days, it seems like hard work is no longer valued. Everyone seems to be looking for the quick-fix, the shortcut or the easy way out. But true success comes from the hard work and smart work needed to build and establish a solid foundation. Work is the currency that purchases success.

If you want to find someone willing to put in the necessary work, look for someone who has a pair of work boots. Primarily worn as protective footwear by construction workers and day laborers, work boots are a staple in the leadership closet; standard issue as part of the uniform for greatness. Work boots are the great equalizers. When everyone on a team is working together, it's difficult to distinguish the leaders from the followers because they all come together and work toward a common goal. When everyone has on work boots, it doesn't matter who gets the credit as long as the job gets done. Work boots thrive in teams because there's an understanding that everyone's role matters and the team rises or falls, fails or succeeds together. TEAM: **T**ogether **E**veryone **A**chieves **M**ore.

Whether you bootstrap an entrepreneurial endeavor to make it work or pull yourself up by your bootstraps, the connotations associated with boots are always about someone who knows how to get the job done. It's crucial to choose the right people for the right jobs –then delegate responsibilities and allow them to do their work. Inherent in leadership is consensus and team-building strategies that foster a sense of mutual respect and trust. If the members of a team do not feel they can trust their leader, it will be difficult to inspire them and almost impossible to lead them.

SHOE BOX # 30
Bronze Baby Shoes & Experience

Why, you may ask, would anyone need a bronze pair of their own baby shoes? In a word: history. Most likely you're familiar with the oft-quoted, "Those who do not learn from history are doomed to repeat it."

Bronze baby shoes are keepsakes from one's childhood to memorialize days gone by. The actual bronzing process applies a conductive material to the shoe surface, and then electroplates a layer of heavy copper onto the shoes to produce a bronze-like surface. Decades ago, a pair of bronze baby shoes for each child could be found in almost every home – a testament to the joyful memories that had already been made.

Bronze baby shoes are reminders. They remind us of the first monumental accomplishment in our lives; learning to walk. They remind us of where we started and how far we've progressed over the years. Since the first uncertain steps that we took as toddlers to the great strides as trailblazing leaders, we've gained a lot of experience in between.

Remember how frustrating it was during your first real job search? Everyone you talked to or interviewed with wanted you to have more experience. Paradoxically, the only way to gain that experience was to convince someone to hire and train you.

Experience is knowledge, skill or practice derived from direct observation or participation in a series of events. Work experience is derived from the accumulation of an individual's various professional endeavors, encounters and accomplishments that develop practical and tangible know-how within specific areas of practice. Experience can be gained from situations which are good, bad or indifferent because they all provide an increased level of education, perspective and various lessons learned. I remember hearing an instructor once say, "Experience is a hard teacher because she gives the test first and the lesson afterward."

SHOE BOX # 31
Valet Shoes & Confidentiality

You are probably asking, 'What are valet shoes?' They are the red-hot (or bottomed), designer, nobody-else-better-have-these-shoes, yet the most uncomfortable and impractical shoes that absolutely make the outfit that you are wearing. You know the ones. Finally, you arrive at the event that you've been planning to attend for months, the door to the Bentley, Benz or limo opens and the first thing out is your valet shoes. Never mind the fact that you had on your driving shoes all the way there. Your valet shoes have a voice all their own. Before you ever open your mouth to introduce yourself – they've already said it all. Your valet shoes are the absolute center of attention. They are the focal point of your ensemble, prompting envious women to whisper just out of earshot; making your girlfriends shake their heads and admit that once again your shoes are off the chain; and encouraging interested men to take a second look.

Although you and your shoes are the highlight of any evening, what people don't know is that you're hiding something. You're hiding the fact that your shoes are killing your feet. The toe box is too pointy and pinches; the heels are too high, causing you to stagger a bit. The truth is you are in pain – although you could never tell by looking.

After the initial, dazzling moments of allowing your valet shoes to be seen, like clockwork, you head to your station for the evening – the place where you can hide your feet, maybe under the banquet table, and take off those sizzling hot, crazy uncomfortable shoes until the next act in your Valet Shoe Play.

The valet shoes you're wearing aren't made to walk in – they're made to be seen in. What people don't know is that although they'll see you all evening, you'll only be in your valet shoes for a matter of minutes; just long enough to make an appearance and to make an impression. As a professional, you understand the value of a well-placed photo opportunity.

On the ride over, you wear well-fitting comfortable and practical shoes out of the house, into the car and to your planned destination. Sometimes, you even wear flats. Shh! You get massages and pedicures before and after wearing your valet shoes to take care of your feet and undo the damage they can cause. People don't know that your valet shoes have their own bag and carrying case because it's more practical and convenient to hold them than to wear them. Your back-up shoes are as much a part of your wardrobe as everything else you're wearing. Back-up shoes make the rest of the evening possible because they make it bearable. But nobody needs to know – because every woman is entitled to have a secret.

And every leader should know and understand the value of confidentiality; the ability to safeguard and treasure those things that should remain unspoken. Often I find that those looking to be led are wounded because the confidences they entrusted in the care of previous leaders were inappropriately shared with others. Be clear and confidential so that those you lead will trust you.

FINISHING TOUCHES

Like any true diva, you will add, toss out and update the shoes and styles in your wardrobe - and in your leadership qualities. However, the 31 pairs discussed herein are a really good start.

As you enhance your leadership closet and expand your shoe collection, remember that it's OK if you don't have all the necessary shoes in the beginning, because on this journey, we're all works in progress. Some shoes may not fit exactly right in the beginning; and others will slide right on and conform to you like a tailored suit. Some shoes you may have to borrow, while others will find their way to you as you encounter the challenges and pathways that require them.

I encourage you to read and memorize some of my favorite quotes, in the section following this one. Take a hard look at your leadership style by using the Leadership Analysis and using that information, along with the tools in this book to identify your professional goals and pursue your aspirations, knowing that you are fully equipped with all the right gear you need to be successful. High-heeled leadership isn't about never failing; it's about never quitting. The truth is that you occasionally may stumble, fall and fail, but the important thing is to keep moving in the direction you want to go. As my mentor Les Brown says, "If you fall, fall on your back; because if you can look up, you can get up." And, as John Maxwell says, "If you must fail, fail forward; because failure is never final as long as you keep trying."

Finally, remember to pass along the lessons you've learned to others who will come behind. True leaders understand that the vision is always bigger than the visionary; and along with blazing trails and shattering glass ceilings, they also accept the responsibility of mentoring and teaching others to lead. Take some time to check out your own closet and find out which shoes are missing, which shoes need to be thrown out, and which ones need to be repaired, replaced or acquired.

It's YOUR time to lead, so let's walk it out!

My 31 Favorite Leadership Quotes

"If the first woman God ever made was strong enough to turn the world upside down all alone, these women together ought to be able to turn it back, and get it right side up again! And now they is asking to do it, the men better let them."

~*Sojourner Truth*

"Perhaps it is impossible for a person who does no good to do no harm."

~*Harriet Beecher Stowe*

"In three words I can sum up everything I've learned about life: it goes on."
~*Robert Frost*

"When I stand before God at the end of my life, I would hope that I would not have a single bit of talent left, and could say, 'I used everything you gave me.'"

~*Erma Bombeck*

"Learn from the mistakes of others. You can't live long enough to make them all yourself."

~*Eleanor Roosevelt*

"Just because something doesn't do what you planned it to do doesn't mean it's useless."

~*Thomas A. Edison*

"Nearly all men can stand adversity, but if you want to test a man's character, give him power."

~*Abraham Lincoln*

"You can't operate a company by fear, because the way to eliminate fear is to avoid criticism. And the way to avoid criticism is to do nothing."

~*Steve Ross*

"Never allow a person to tell you 'no' who doesn't have the power to say 'yes'."

~*Eleanor Roosevelt*

"If women are expected to do the same work as men, we must teach them the same things."

~*Plato*

"However beautiful the strategy, you should occasionally look at the results."

~*Sir Winston Churchill*

"People are like stained-glass windows. They sparkle and shine when the sun is out, but when the darkness sets in, their true beauty is revealed only if there is a light from within."

~*Elizabeth Kubler Ross*

"The journey is the reward."

~*Chinese Proverb*

"In politics if you want anything said, ask a man. If you want anything done, ask a woman."

~*Margaret Thatcher*

"One cannot consent to creep when one has an impulse to soar."

~*Helen Keller*

"I do not pray for success. I ask for faithfulness."

~*Mother Teresa*

"Success is the ability to go from failure to failure without losing your enthusiasm."

~*Sir Winston Churchill*

"You may have to fight a battle more than once to win it."

~*Margaret Thatcher*

"I only want people around me who can do the impossible."

~*Elizabeth Arden*

"I don't measure a man's success by how high he climbs but how high he bounces when he hits bottom."
~*General George S. Patton*

"I don't know the key to success, but the key to failure is trying to please everybody."
~*Bill Cosby*

"A stumble may prevent a fall."
~*English Proverb*

"I honestly think it is better to be a failure at something you love than to be a success at something you hate."
~*George Burns*

"In order to succeed, your desire for success should be greater than your fear of failure."
~*Bill Cosby*

"What you are must always displease you, if you would attain to that which you are not."
~*Saint Augustine*

"Common sense in an uncommon degree is what the world calls wisdom."
~*Samuel Taylor Coleridge*

"Being powerful is like being a lady. If you have to tell people you are, you aren't."
~*Margaret Thatcher*

"I'll try anything once, twice if I like it, three times to make sure."
~*Mae West*

"Passion is the genesis of genius."
~*Tony Robbins*

"There is no passion to be found playing small - in settling for a life that is less than the one you are capable of living."

~Nelson Mandela

"You cannot depend on your eyes when your imagination is out of focus."

~Mark Twain

"The greatest danger for most of us is not that our aim is too high and we miss it, but that it is too low and we reach it."

`~Michelangelo

Footnotes: Leadership Analyses

Use this portion of the book to discover your strengths and areas for improvement in your personal leadership style.

Footnotes: Leadership Analysis #1

Who are the women that you admire and would like to pattern your success after? Why do you admire them? List at least five women leaders and what you most admire about them below:

1. _____

_____

2. _____

_____

3. _____

_____

4. _____

_____

5. _____

_____

Footnotes: Leadership Analysis #2

What is your ultimate leadership goal? Consider the steps necessary to accomplish it and list them below:

1. _____

_____

2. _____

_____

3. _____

_____

4. _____

_____

5. _____

_____

Footnotes: Leadership Analysis #3

Of the 31 leadership qualities highlighted in this book, which five are your strongest?

1. _____

_____

2. _____

_____

3. _____

_____

4. _____

_____

5. _____

_____

Footnotes: Leadership Analysis #4

Of the 31 leadership qualities highlighted in this book, which ones do you need to develop most?

1. _____

_____

2. _____

_____

3. _____

_____

4. _____

_____

5. _____

_____

Footnotes: Leadership Analysis #5

Describe where you see yourself and what you see yourself doing in 5 years:

Year 1. _____

_____

Year 2. _____

_____

Year 3._____

_____

Year 4. _____

_____

Year 5._____

_____

Footnotes: Leadership Analysis #6

Describe the achievement for which you are proudest:

_____

_____

_____

_____

Footnotes: Leadership Analysis #7

List five tangible steps you can take to enhance your leadership skills:

1. _____

_____

2. _____

_____

3. _____

_____

4. _____

_____

5. _____

_____

Footnotes: Leadership Analysis #8

What new skills or experiences would you like to acquire to improve your leadership qualifications?

1. _____

_____

2. _____

_____

3. _____

_____

4. _____

_____

5. _____

_____

Footnotes: Leadership Analysis #9

Describe the leadership qualities of the two women closest to you and consider whether they help or hinder your professional progress.

1. _____

_____

2. _____

_____

3. _____

_____

4. _____

_____

5. _____

_____

Footnotes: Leadership Analysis #10

Describe your favorite pair of shoes – and how you feel when you wear them:

_____

_____

_____

_____

ABOUT KATRINA FERGUSON

Katrina Ferguson, entrepreneur, author, speaker, life coach and philanthropist, accredits her success to determination, ambition and a constantly evolving "why". Ms. Ferguson is the founder of the **Total Woman Workshop**, a workshop series designed to foster self awareness, personal and spiritual growth. Whether you seek empowerment in the areas of fitness, finances, faith, focus, follow-thru or any other, you will be blessed, inspired and empowered by Ms. Ferguson's trainings.

Ms. Ferguson has been featured in many publications, including *Essence* and *Success From Home Magazines, Why Can't We Say What we Mean, The Urban Connection and Walking with the Wise Entrepreneur*, as well as having been a guest on numerous radio appearances and interviews. She has spoken at events all around the world, in front of audiences of over 15,000 members. She is the visionary and author of several books including, _Celebrate the Power in Your Right to Choose_ and _The Queens' Legacy_, released under her personal publishing company label.

Ms. Ferguson has created a following of women through her workshop and the direct sales market, seeking to gain security in their finances, faith, focus and follow-through. Her ultimate goal through all of her ventures is to help people realize their potential and grow pass all limitations.

Ms. Ferguson is quoted saying, "If Your Why is Big Enough, the Hows will Take Care of Themselves". Her trainings and events include sharing tools for success, secrets of determination, spiritual guidance and tips to unlock your "why" for personal empowerment and living on purpose.

For more information, to purchase Ms. Ferguson's materials or to request an appearance, please contact her at 888.202.6766 or visit her website www.TheTotalWomanWorkshop.com or www.KatrinaSpeaks.com

The Total Woman Workshop

PRESENTS

COACHING
Katrina Ferguson's Way

COACHING INCLUDES:

TWO - ONE HOUR GROUP COACHING SESSIONS
24 /7 ONLINE ACCESS TO ONLINE COACHING LIBRARY
PERSONAL WORKBOOKS TO USE DURING COACHING CALLS
COACHING IN AREAS INCLUDING:

- FAITH
- FITNESS
- FINANCE
- FOCUS
- FOLLOW-THROUGH
- AND MORE!!

YOUR OWN COPY OF BOOKS FROM KATRINA'S SUCCESS LIBRARY INCLUDING

- THE QUEEN'S LEGACY
- WALKING WITH THE WISE ENTREPRENEUR
- CELEBRATE THE POWER IN YOUR RIGHT TO CHOOSE
- REMODEL YOUR REALITY

E-BOOK COLLECTION

- AS A WOMAN THINKETH
- THE SCIENCE OF GETTING RICH

AND MORE

VALUE: $249 PER MONTH
FOOTNOTES SPECIAL: $147 FIRST MONTH
$97 EACH ADDITIONAL MONTH
MINIMUM THREE MONTH COMMITMENT

TO REGISTER OR FOR MORE INFORMATION CONTACT:
1-888-202-6766
WWW.THETOTALWOMANWORKSHOP.COM
INFO@THETOTALWOMANWORKSHOP.COM

Other Titles by Katrina Ferguson

9 780982 818008